WHITE WEDDING

A Homely Comedy in One Act

by
TERENCE BOWEN

SAMUEL FRENCH LIMITED
LONDON

SAMUEL FRENCH LTD
26 SOUTHAMPTON STREET, STRAND, LONDON, W.C.2

SAMUEL FRENCH INC.
25 WEST 45TH STREET, NEW YORK, U.S.A.
7623 SUNSET BOULEVARD, HOLLYWOOD 46, CAL.

SAMUEL FRENCH (CANADA) LTD
27 GRENVILLE STREET, TORONTO

SAMUEL FRENCH (AUSTRALIA) PTY LTD
159 FORBES STREET, SYDNEY

MADE AND PRINTED IN GREAT BRITAIN BY
BUTLER & TANNER LTD, FROME AND LONDON
MADE IN ENGLAND

CHARACTERS

(in Order of Appearance.)

MUM MASON	..	(Aged 45)
DAD MASON	..	(Aged 50)
MAVIS MASON	..	(Aged 14)
POLLY HAWTRIPP	..	(Aged 16)
GWEN MASON	..	(Aged 23)
MRS BAGSHAW	..	(Aged 70)
TOM OSBORNE	..	(Aged 27)

(PODGER the dog is not mentioned in the list of characters because the author feels that an intimation of his appearance may well spoil the final curtain of the play.)

SCENE.—*The Mason's living room.*

TIME.—*A Spring morning.*

iii

WHITE WEDDING

SCENE: *The living-room of the* MASONS' *house, in a Northern industrial town. A Spring morning.*

This kitchen-cum-living room is comfortably, cheerfully furnished but a little overcrowded. There are three doors. One, at the back, R.C., *leads to the street. Another, up stage in the* R. *wall, to the kitchen. The third, down stage in the* R. *wall, to the hall, staircase, and front door. The window is at the back,* C. *Against the* R. *wall, between the two doors is a sideboard, with the usual dressings, a vase of flowers, and, above it, a mirror. The fireplace is at* L., *with an armchair above it and a small easy chair below. There is a small table at* C., *with two chairs,* R. *and* L. *of it. Two more small chairs are placed at the back, on either side of the window. An occasional table, above the armchair, another table or a cupboard up* L., *may complete the furniture, but a sofa may be added, if desired, in front of the window.*

On the mantel-piece, in addition to the clock, ornaments, and a match-holder, is a small jeweller's box. On the table is a florist's box containing a bridal bouquet, a bridesmaid's bouquet, and a floral shoulder spray. Next to this is another box containing MRS MASON'S *new hat.*

(*See the Ground Plan at the end of the Play.*)

Before the CURTAIN *rises, a dog howls piteously.*

When the CURTAIN *rises,* MRS MASON (" MUM ") *is at the window, peering dejectedly out at the rain. She wears a costume and a fussy blouse.* MR MASON (" DAD ") *is standing by the chair* L. *of the table, facing front, and polishing his already shining boots, with one foot on the chair. He is in shirt*

1

*sleeves, his coat on the back of the chair. He is a
meek, kindly man. MUM is neither very kindly
nor meek. They are in the late forties. The dog
howls again—presumably from the back-yard.*

DAD. What a morning ! Raining cats and dogs.

MUM. I wish our dog would stop howling. Most
unlucky. Wouldn't it just pour down today for
the wedding ?

DAD. It'll do good to the gardens, Mother.

MUM. The gardens be blowed. What was weather
report on wireless this morning ?

DAD. I dunno. I was too busy getting the
breakfast to notice.

MUM. Good job you don't have to do it every
morning. (*She rises, and moves down* R.C. *In her
hair waves are two metal clamps. She takes these
out in front of the mirror and puts them in the sideboard drawer.*)

MUM. Paying all that brass to have my hair
set—it'll be as straight as straw before we reach the
church if this weather keeps up.

DAD. Before we were wed I thought your hair
were naturally curly.

MUM. Aye. And I thought you were earning
good money. Still, there won't be no eyes on me
when they see our Gwennie as a white bride. She'll
be looking like an angel, bless her (*crossing to the
door down* R.) like an angel. (*In complete contrast,
she opens the door and bellows.*) Gwennie !

GWEN (*off*). Yes ?

MUM. Want any help, love ?

GWEN. No, ta !

(*During this* DAD *has finished his shoes and is now
sitting on the chair with folded arms.*)

MUM. All right, then. Be independent. (*Moving
to* R. *of the table.*) She'll be calling for her Mother
soon enough, I dare swear. (*She takes her hat out of*

the box carefully. It is a gay confection of flowers and ribbon.) My wedding hat ! If I'd known what weather were going to be like I'd have bought a sou'wester.

DAD. You're never going to wear that—that article ?

MUM. Why ? Don't you think it will suit me ?

DAD (*rather nervously*). Well—no, love.

MUM. Then it's sure to be all right. Are you leaning back on your coat ? (*She puts down her hat and crosses above the table to him.*)

DAD (*straightening up quickly*). No, love.

MUM (L. *of* DAD : *pushing him forward*). You daft 'aporth ! (*Picking up his coat.*) You've crushed your posy. (*Rearranging it.*) Can't even look decent for your eldest daughter's wedding. Come on ! Get this coat on and you'll be one finished with. (*She helps him to put his coat on.*) I can't think how our poor Gwen's doing with Mavis and Cousin Polly. Bridesmaids are always bunglers. There !

(DAD *crosses* L. *and sits above the fireplace.*)

I've a good mind to go up to her. (*She moves above the table.*)

DAD. Best not. Anyhow, (*glancing at the door down* R.) someone's coming down—

(MAVIS MASON *enters. She is a buxom fourteen year old, most unsuitably dressed in a short sleeved, long pastel shade frock and a rather unsecure head-dress of flowers, and comes in doing a stately march as she hums the Wedding March. She pays no attention to her parents but proceeds her slow way up* R., *to the back kitchen door.*)

MUM (*watching her*). The voice that breathed o'er Eden ! Where do you think you're going, Mavis ?

MAVIS. Glass of water, Mum. Wouldn't it be thrilling if bridegroom didn't turn up ?

(She exits up R.*)*

MUM. Saucy madam. She's been going to the pictures too much. (*As she moves up to the window.*) It looks set in for the day. And only yesterday Betty Ramsbottom had blazing sunshine and her in a tailor made. (*Ironically.*) "Happy is the bride that the sun shines on—" (*She moves down to the table and commences to put on her hat.*)

DAD. Remember our wedding day? I nearly 'ad sunstroke.

MUM. Which only goes to show you can't pin much faith in these old sayings.

DAD. Nay, nay, Mother. I've always done my level best to make you happy—

MUM. And what a very level sort of best it's been. Scraping and saving and doing without ever since we was wed. That's why I was determined our Gwen wasn't going to chuck herself away on a poor chap. It's been a bit of an eye-opener round here, her going to wed Seth Orwell's only son.

DAD. Seth Orwell's none too popular, remember.

MUM. Of course, he's not. *He's* got on. Went to same school as the lot of you—and now he's got two shops and a row of houses. I tell you, Will Mason, nowadays it's money that talks.

DAD (*grinning*). Seth doesn't let his talk too much. And I reckon his lad takes after him.

MUM. There's sense in being careful when you've got it. I admit Jack's not half the chap his father was but you'll see the difference when he's got our Gwen behind him. It's what a lot of men need. A woman behind them—pushing them forward.

DAD (*sadly*). I know.

MUM. Even if Jack hasn't inherited his father's character—he's going to inherit his money.

(MAVIS *saunters in carrying a glass of water which she absent mindedly drinks during the following.*)

MUM. Come here, Mavis, your bandeau's cock-eyed. (*She arranges the head-dress.*) If you can't make yourself look decent I don't know what bride will look like. Who's the water for?

MAVIS (R.C.). Cousin Polly. Got one of her sick headaches coming on—she looks terrible.

MUM. A pity *she* can't wear a veil—and a good thick 'un.

(*The dog howls in the back yard.*)

MUM. That dratted dog of yours. I'll wring his neck.

MAVIS. Poor old Podger. He's heard my voice. Mum, can't I please take him to the wedding?

MUM. For the two hundred and fiftieth time—no!

MAVIS. There was a picture in the paper of a bride who had a pack of hounds at her's. (*She moves up to the window.*)

MUM. Well, we're having your Dad's relations instead. Remember now, Podger stays in the wash-house till after reception. Run along with that water.

MAVIS (*turning; in wonderment*). Eh—I've gone and drunk it. (*Crossing to the kitchen, petulantly.*) Gwen would go and fix her wedding for same day as Heckleydown Dog Show.

(*She exits.*)

MUM. Heckleydown Dog Show! That's all she thinks on. When Gwen walks down the aisle with these two bridesmaids it'll put folk in mind of Cinder-ella and her Ugly Sisters. There'll be Mavis dreaming of a Dog Show and Cousin Polly looking as if she'd escaped from one—her usual washed-out picture of perfect misery—

(*During the last sentence* DAD *signals violently to stop her, for* COUSIN POLLY *has drifted in down* R. *She is a tall, thin, pale sixteen, angular and slow in her movements. She wears a similar outfit to Mavis'.*)

MUM (*turning ; with an immediate change of tone*). Why, Polly, love. I was just saying to your Uncle what a picture you and Mavis were going to make, to be sure.

POLLY (*down* R.). Has Mavis got my water ?

MUM. I'll water her. (*She goes up* R. *to the kitchen door.*)

DAD. How are you feeling, Polly ?

POLLY (*moving to above the table*). Only sort of so so, Uncle Willie.

MUM (*calling through the doorway*). Mavis, get your head in out of the rain this minute ! What do you think you're up to ?

(MAVIS *comes in with the glass of water.*)

MAVIS (*moving down* R.C.). Podger's got his little pink nose stuck under door, miserable like— (*She gives the glass to* POLLY.)

MUM (*moving to* C.). That's no reason for you to have your big, fat head stuck out of window, stupid like. Drink it up, Polly—you're not a hen.

POLLY (*having sipped the water*). I hope I can keep it down. (*She eases to* L. *of the table.*)

MUM. We don't want no regrettable incidents in Church, remember. And get your jersey put on. Your arms are blue with cold.

(POLLY *puts the glass on the table and looks at her arms.*)

POLLY. Mother says it's a pity you didn't choose long sleeves. (*Waving her arms dreamily.*) She says these favour match sticks.

MUM. Match sticks ! That reminds me. I haven't given you girls the bridegroom's gifts. Will, get that little box off mantelshelf—behind the matches. Buck up ! Get weaving !

(DAD *rises, takes the box from the mantel and brings it to* C., *above the table.*)

POLLY. " Bridegroom to Bridesmaids. Gold Bracelets.'' Thats what you sent to the *Gazette*, isn't it, Auntie ? I've never had anything gold before.

MAVIS. They don't like us to wear jewellery in the Guides. I hope they're not too fancy. Hurry up, Dad.

(DAD *has the box on the table. They cluster excitedly round. He holds up two exceedingly narrow gold chain bracelets.* MUM *takes them and gives one each to the girls.*)

MUM. Solid gold. Aren't you lucky, girls ?

(*There is a distinct cooling off in the excitement.*)

MAVIS. They don't look very solid—nor very gold, neither.

MUM. For shame on you, our Mavis. Jack Orwell had them made special. Let me help you with the clasp, Polly.

MAVIS. I know mine will never go round. (*She sits,* R. *of the table.*) Jack Orwell hasn't half skimped the solid gold—

(*During* MAVIS' *speech,* GWEN *enters down* R., *her bridal dress not fastened down the back. It is very simple and she is not wearing her veil. She is twenty-three and very pretty. The others do not see her. She stands by the door, and watches them with amusement.*)

POLLY. Sort of old fashioned, aren't they ?

MUM. Valuable antiques, doubtless. Is there a card in the box, Will ? Something the girls can have for a keepsake ?

DAD. There's a paper here. (*He reads.*) " To cutting old gold chain and providing two gilt clasps. One pound, three shillings and . . . '' (*He looks up.*) Why, Gwen, love !

*

(The others turn.)

GWEN *(gaily)*. His Grannie's gold chain. Careful family, the Orwells.

MUM. Gwen, you're not even fastened. *(Easing to R. of the table.)* Come over here.

(GWEN obeys.)

Careful you don't catch your dress, now. What's brought you down? *(She commences to fasten the dress.)*

GWEN. Looking for my ladies-in-waiting. Ow, your fingers are like ice, Mum. Feeling better, Polly?

POLLY. Sick as a dog—

MAVIS *(quickly)*. Talking of dogs, Gwen—

GWEN *(cutting in)*. No! You cannot bring Podger to my wedding! If anyone's going to howl outside the church, it's going to be *me*. *(To MUM.)* Thanks, Mum. *(Moving down R.)* Come on, stooges, and help me fix my veil.

(MAVIS and POLLY move towards R.C. DAD moves L., to the armchair above the fire, and sits.)

MUM *(at R.C. : a trifle pathetically)*. Let me come, love.

GWEN. Please, Mum. You only make me nervous.

MUM. Nervous? What about? You look a picture. There won't be a prouder man in England this day than Jack Orwell.

GWEN. Oh—*damn* Jack Orwell!

MUM. That's a nice thing for the future Mrs Jack Orwell to be saying, I'm sure!

GWEN. Jack Orwell this—Jack Orwell that—I'm sick of the name, I tell you. I'm sick of it all. I wish I were dead. Dead! Dead! Dead!

(Weeping, she rushes off down R. MUM takes charge of the situation like a General marshalling his troops.)

MUM. Mavis ! Up those stairs after her and see she doesn't flop on the bed in her wedding dress.

(MAVIS *gives a Girl Guide salute, lifts up her long dress, and dashes off in hot pursuit.*)

Polly ! Oh—you go into back kitchen and take a headache powder. They're in sweet bottle over the sink. And look lively !

(POLLY *goes off quite quickly for her, carrying the empty glass.*)

Dad !

DAD (*springing to his feet*). Aye, aye !

MUM (*at a loss*). Er—sit down.

(DAD *obeys.* MUM *sits* R. *of the table, carefully hitching up her skirt as she does so.*)

I don't know, Will ! I always thought our Gwen was one of your sensible sort.

DAD. Perhaps she doesn't want to marry Jack Orwell.

MUM. She doesn't know what she wants. Girls at her age never do. (*She sighs.*) I wish I'd listened to *my* Mother.

DAD. Your Mother ? As far as she's concerned I'm still " I told you so." (*He thinks for a moment.*) Bessie—you don't think our Gwen is still fretting over Tom Osborne ?

MUM (*contemptuously*). Tom Osborne ! What a match he'd have made for the lass. A twopenny 'apenny bit of a joiner and never in a steady job five minutes together. Don't you bring *him* up again !

DAD. Now, you know you've always been prejudiced because his Uncle George jilted your Florrie before our Gwen were thought of.

MUM. Just as Tom Osborne would have back worded our Gwen if I hadn't nipped that little romance in the bud double quick. Remember how he used to be meeting her on the sly—

DAD (*quickly*). You never gave them a chance to do owt else—

MUM (*ignoring him*). And then he gets a job out of town and leaves her flat. Unstable—like all the Osbornes.

DAD (*rising, and moving idly to the window*). I thought he was a likely enough lad—and so did our Gwen.

MUM. She were just at the age to fall in love with a pair of blue eyes and no prospects. It soon learned her her lesson him going off to Scotland —and not so much as a postcard from him this six months or more.

(DAD *turns, and moves down* L. *of the table.*)

DAD. Are you dead certain on that, Bessie?

MUM (*turning to look at him*). What are you looking at me like that for? (*A slight pause.*) What do you mean—dead certain?

DAD. One morning, a two-three weeks after Tom Osborne went away, the post came before I'd gone to work and there was a letter for Gwen—from Scotland. She never mentioned it and I've always kind of wondered . . . (*He breaks off still looking at her.*)

(MUM *rises, moves* R.C., *and commences to pin her shoulder spray on her coat with an affectation of complete unconcern.*)

MUM. Wondered what, Will Mason?

DAD (*losing his nerve*). Wondered—well—if it was from Tom—and—and . . .

MUM. And . . . ?

DAD (*moving away towards the fire*). And it got mislaid or summat.

MUM. Are you insinuating that I destroyed a letter belonging to someone else in this house?

DAD (*easing down* L.). I never said you destroyed it.

Mum (*moving quickly to* L.C., *below the table*). I suppose it jumped off the mantelshelf into the fire on its own ? There never was no letter—d'you understand, Will Mason ? And if I hear any more from you—

(*The dog barks off stage.* POLLY *comes quietly in from the back kitchen, the door of which she has left ajar during the above conversation.*)

POLLY (*loudly*). Auntie !
MUM (*swinging round*). You gave me quite a turn ! Don't come sneaking in here like that. What's to do ?
POLLY (*up* R.). There's a lady coming up the yard with an umbrella.
MUM. What do you expect her to be carrying on a day like this —a parasol ?

(*There is a knock on the back door.*)

Go on, gormless, *open* it !

(POLLY *does so. Outside is an elderly woman with a dripping mackintosh over her head and an umbrella. This is* MRS BAGSHAW *from " down the street."*)

MUM. Why, Mrs Bagshaw ! Come in out of the wet.
MRS BAGSHAW (*moving to below the doorway*). No further than the mat, Bessie, or I'll flood the house. What a day, to be sure. Why, Polly Hawtripp, you gave me quite a start. Don't know about a wedding— you look pale enough for a funeral.
MUM. She's nervous. Never been a bridesmaid before.

(POLLY *turns slowly down* L. *and sits by the fire.*)

MRS BAGSHAW. She looks the sort as will do it plenty. It's your Mother I've come about.

MUM. There's nowt wrong?

MRS BAGSHAW (*chuckling*). She wants you to come and fasten her dress. Her hands are trembling something shocking. And I've broken me glasses and can't see the hooks from the eyes.

MUM (*up* C.). I'm not going in this downpour. Dad, you'll have to go.

DAD. Me do up your Mother's dress? I'd as soon fasten a wolf in sheep's clothing.

(MUM *wheels round looking for* POLLY.)

MUM. Then that only leaves—

POLLY (*quickly*). The Doctor says the only cure for my headaches is to sit still for ten minutes and do nowt.

MUM. Then all I can say is that most of your family must never have been without 'em. I can't go like this Dad!

DAD (*looking at his watch*). I've got to take up sentry-go at the end of street to watch for bridegroom's taxi, and give our Gwen the starting signal.

MRS BAGSHAW (*a trifle acidly*). And it would never do to let Mr Jack Orwell slip through your fingers.

MUM. Oh, botheration! (*Crossing down* R.) I'll borrow your big mack, Dad.

DAD. 'Ere! I don't want to go to wedding all wet.

MUM. You were all wet to begin with.

(*She exits.*)

MRS BAGSHAW (*with meaning*). I'll bet you've cause to remember your wedding day, Will.

DAD. She's a bit on edge. Worrying for Gwen, you know.

MRS BAGSHAW (*moving down a little*, R.C.). Every woman worries when her daughters get wed—but

they worry a darn sight more when they don't. Tell
me, Will. Wasn't your Gwennie a bit sweet on Tom
Osborne, once over?

DAD (*hurrying to her, fingers on lips*). Ss'h! His
name's a red rag to her . . . (*He makes a gesture
towards the stairs.*)

MRS BAGSHAW (*in a stage whisper*). He's back in
town, tha knows.

(POLLY *comes out of her trance and listens eagerly.*)

DAD. Tom Osborne back? He's *never*!

MRS BAGSHAW. Been back since Sunday. Proper
cut up about this wedding, they say. I do 'ope for
all your sakes 'e doesn't turn up at the Church and
do something violent. (*Her tone, alas, implies just
the opposite.* MRS BAGSHAW *has not been invited to
the reception.*)

MUM (*calling; off stage*). Gwen, I'm just round
to your Grannie's for a minute.

DAD (*to* MRS BAGSHAW). Not a word—remember!

MRS BAGSHAW. Cross me heart. I've too much
respect for her Mother.

(MUM *bustles in. Over her shoulders she has slung*
DAD's *mack. Her hat has been replaced with a
plastic " pixie ", and she carries a modern umbrella
in several gaudy shades.*)

MUM. I'll share your brolly, Mrs Bagshaw, and
Dad can have our Mavis' new one. (*She gives it
to him.*)

(MRS BAGSHAW *steps out of the back door, and puts
up her umbrella.* MUM *follows her.* DAD *looks
aghast at his umbrella.*)

DAD. 'Ere! What am I supposed to do wi'
this Japanese sunshade?

MUM (*turning on the doorstep*). Hold it in your right hand—and jump off suspension bridge.

(*She goes off, banging the door behind her.*)

DAD. Hell-as-like, I'll not. (*He opens it gingerly.*)
POLLY. It's unlucky to open umbrella in the house.
DAD. It'll be more unlucky if I open it outside. What if I meet one of my mates ?

(*A doorbell rings off* R.)

DAD. The front bell !
POLLY. Fellers carry them brighter than that on Golf Links.
DAD. Aye. And on top of elephants in India. Go on, Polly ! Answer front door, there's a good lass.

(POLLY *rises, and moves towards the door down* R., *with little enthusiasm.*)

POLLY. I still feel peculiar.
DAD (*moving to the door at the back*). Well, the walk'll do you good.

(POLLY *exits* R. DAD *cautiously opens the back door and peers out. He turns up his coat collar and disgustedly opens the umbrella.* MAVIS *runs in down* R.)

MAVIS. Where are you going with my birthday umbrella ?
DAD. Golfing !

(*He disappears quickly from view, off* R. MAVIS *runs up to the back door and peers after him. She then shrugs her shoulders and closes the door.* POLLY *comes in* R. *and crosses to the table. She carries a bunch of violets in cellophane.*)

MAVIS (*moving down*).   Who was at front door ?

POLLY.   Lad from flower shop with these violets.

MAVIS (*almost snatching them from her*).   Violets !
Gosh !   What time do you make it ?   (*She begins
to unwrap the violets.*)

POLLY.   Getting on for twenty to.   Hey, those are
for your Gwen.

MAVIS.   I know.   Eh, the silly fool's forgotten
to put a card in—and I told him—

(GWEN, *radiant in wreath and veil, enters down* R.)

POLLY (*crossing* L., *below the table*).   They're half
mourning.   Fancy sending a bride violets.

GWEN.   Violets !   (*She rushes to the table and
picks up the flowers.*)   There's only Tom Osborne
would send me violets.   Bless the lad !   How did
they come ?   By post ?

POLLY.   No.   From flower shop next to Market.
Tom Osborne's back in town.

GWEN (*putting down violets*).   What did you say ?

POLLY.   Mrs Bagshaw was telling your Dad a
minute since.   Tom Osborne's been back since Mon-
day.

GWEN (*turning away tearfully*).   And he's never
tried to see me.   To wish me—happiness.   I suppose
if I wasn't good enough to write to when he was
away . . . (*She breaks off.*)

POLLY (*below and* L. *of the table*).   That's just what
your Dad and Mum were having words over.   He was
accusing her of destroying some letter as Tom Osborne
had wrote you, and—

(GWEN *crosses, and seizes her by the shoulders.*)

GWEN.   Is that the truth, Polly ?   Is that the gospel
truth ?

POLLY.   Let me go !   You'll start my head off
again !

GWEN.   I'll *shake* it off if you don't tell me—

POLLY (*cutting in*). Your Dad said she burned a
letter from Scotland so you shouldn't see it—
    GWEN. Oh! (*To* POLLY, *dropping her hands.*)
Sorry, love. (*She crosses wearily to* L. *of the table
and sits.*) I don't know how she could. My own
Mother. I don't know how anyone could be so
cruel. (*She buries her head in her hands.*)

(*The two girls gaze at her tenderly. The dog barks—
    just once. This galvanizes* MAVIS *into action. She
    might almost have been expecting it.*)

MAVIS (*moving towards* POLLY). The only way
to cure your headache, Polly, is to lie down for ten
minutes in the parlour.
    POLLY. I'll crease my frock—
    MAVIS (*cutting in*). I'll crease you if you don't.
Get on with you. (*She commences to propel her
along by force, towards down* R.)
    POLLY (*as they go across*). I tell you I don't want
to lie down—ow—you're pinching—*ow* . . .

(MAVIS *pushes her off* R. *and one hears her complaints
    until a door slams. Somebody whistles—two notes—
    from the yard.* GWEN *looks up.* MAVIS *dashes in
    brandishing a key which she puts on the sideboard.*)

MAVIS. There! (*Showing the key.*) I've locked
her in.
    GWEN. Whatever for?
    MAVIS. To keep her out of the way.

(*She crosses towards the window, humming the Wedding
    March with a nonchalance that would deceive no
    one. She peers out, watched by a wondering* GWEN.
    MAVIS *opens the back door and whistles twice.*)

GWEN. What on earth . . . ?
    MAVIS. Just seeing if rain has stopped—
    GWEN. And has it?

MAVIS. Not yet. (*She moves from the back door to the kitchen door.*) But they always have it fine—for Heckleydown Dog Show !

(*She exits.* GWEN *shrugs her shoulders in amazement, picks up the violets tenderly, and holds them to her face.*)

GWEN (*softly*). Oh, Tom lad . . .

(*She has her back to the back door. It opens quietly, and* TOM, *a good looking young man, peers round stealthily. He steps in and closes the door. He wears a mackintosh—very wet—and a hat. He takes off his hat, looks at* GWEN *kissing the violets, and grins.*)

TOM. How do ?

GWEN (*springing up and turning in alarm*). Oh! Tom Osborne ! (*She becomes conscious she is holding the flowers and flings them back on the table.*) You must be crazy.

TOM. If what I hear is true I'm not the only crazy one in these parts. (*He is very much at ease.*)

GWEN (*below and* L. *of the table ; nervously*). What do you mean ?

TOM. Aren't you going to marry that spineless Jack Orwell this morning for his—well, for his Dad's money ?

GWEN (*angrily*). And what right have you got to question me, Tom Osborne ? I'll marry who I please—when I please—and where I please.

TOM (*moving down* R.C.). When I went away, you said you'd wait. (*Crossing to her.*) Have you forgotten that, Gwen ?

GWEN (*retreating*). Don't you dare come near me. You're—you're absolutely soaked. My dress—you know.

TOM. That's easy remedied. (*He takes off his coat and moves up to the kitchen door.*) Nasty morning,

isn't it? The worst sort of day for a wedding.
(*Hanging up his hat and coat.*) The weather's almost
as much of a drip as the bridegroom you've chose.
(*He moves down towards her, unhurriedly.*)

GWEN. You're a fine one to talk. And you
keep your distance.

TOM (*down* C.). We haven't seen each other for
quite a while, Gwen. All I want's a kiss—

(GWEN *retreats backwards right round the table not
daring to take her eyes off him. He follows. She
cannot guess at his mood. Finally she backs into
the chair* R. *of the table, and stands helplessly. He
advances on her and holds out his arms.*)

GWEN. I'll scream—
TOM. Scream away.

(*He embraces her. She does not resist.*)

Go on. Scream. (*Very deliberately he kisses her.*)

(*She returns his kiss and then pushes him away gently.
There are tears in her voice.*)

GWEN. Tom, lad, why didn't you write? (*She
moves away, below the table.*)

TOM. I did. And you never answered one.

GWEN. Then Polly was right. Mum did destroy
them . . . (*She breaks off, and stares out.*)

TOM. Your Ma never did exactly approve, did
she?

GWEN (*looking at him*). And I hadn't your
address—

TOM (*cutting in*). You could have easy found out.

GWEN. I was—too proud. (*She looks away.*)
And when I didn't hear and the months slipped by,
I thought Mum was right and you'd never really
cared—not serious, like. (*Her head droops.*)

(TOM *moves to her, raises her head, and looks into her eyes.*)

TOM. Could you ever have believed that, Gwennie ?

GWEN (*hurriedly*). And one night after a dance, Jack Orwell brought me home in his car—and—and—

TOM. And your Ma approved all right, I suppose. Do you—love him, Gwen ?

GWEN. I'm marrying him in about twenty minutes.

TOM. I said—do—you—*love* him ?

GWEN. He'll make a good, steady husband. He's got wonderful prospects—and——(*She moves away to the fire, and stares down at it.*)

TOM (*at* C.). And I'm not much good, I suppose ? I never have been steady, eh ? And when my old man dies there'll be nowt but the club money. But I love you, Gwen, with all my heart—and you love me, too, don't you ?

GWEN (*turning*). It isn't fair of you to come here and talk like this. (*Moving slowly towards him.*) It's too late, Tom—too late. (*She checks at* L.C.)

TOM. It's not too late to tell you a few things I tried to say in my letters. I've got a good job in Scotland, Gwen—and it's steady—and there's wonderful prospects and all.

GWEN (*turning, moving away to the armchair above the fire*). I'm sure I'm very glad, Tom. For your sake.

TOM. I'm the resident joiner to a Dog Track.

GWEN (*smiling wanly*). Dog Track ? Mum won't approve of that.

TOM. There's one person in this house who does. The minute I said " Dog Track ", she said she'd fix it so I saw you this morning—

GWEN (*swinging round*). You don't mean our Mavis has . . . ?

TOM. She's a sport, your kid. Of course I had to promise her a job as kennel maid. (*Attempting a Scots accent.*) There's a wee spare room for her in our hoose, ye ken.

GWEN. In our *what*?

TOM. Hoose—House! There's one goes with the job. And I've got a special licence and made the arrangements at the Registry Office—

GWEN. Arrangements for what?

TOM. For our wedding this morning, of course.

(GWEN *stares at him. A slight pause.*)

GWEN. Do you think I'm going to make my family the laughing stock of Harbiggen? Do you think I'm going to keep poor Jack Orwell waiting at—?

TOM (*looking at his watch*). You'd better get cracking. You bag is packed, I suppose?

GWEN. I'm marrying Jack Orwell, I tell you! The banns have been called, the reception's been ordered—

TOM. I'm sorry I wasn't here long enough for banns, love—but we can always use the reception.

(*A knocking is heard off* R. *They pay no attention to it.*)

GWEN. I wouldn't marry you if you were the last man left on earth. (*She is beginning to lose her temper.*)

TOM. You wouldn't be able to. There'd be no man left to wed us. (*He laughs.*)

GWEN (*exasperated*). Oh—you—you . . .

TOM. Naughty temper!

(*He takes her in his arms and kisses her as she struggles.* MAVIS *runs in* R.)

MAVIS. Out of the clinch! Mum's coming! (*She points up stage to the back door.*)

GWEN. Tom! She mustn't see you! (*To* MAVIS.) Where can we hide him? The parlour?

(*The knocking re-commences.*)

MAVIS. Polly's in there. Knocking to come out.

GWEN. Take him up to our room, and hide him in the wardrobe.

(TOM *fetches his hat and coat from the peg on the kitchen door.* MAVIS *dashes off, down* R. TOM *follows, pauses in the doorway, and calls to* GWEN.)

TOM. If I'm caught up there—you'll *have* to marry me !

(*He blows her a kiss and exits.* GWEN, L. *of the table, takes out her bouquet, as* MUM *enters up* R.C., *carrying her raincoat and* " *pixie* ".)

MUM. The rain's giving over at last, thank heaven. There's too much fern in that bouquet—it looks like a salad. (*Glancing at the clock.*) Oh, look at the time ! (*She crosses down* R.)

GWEN (*alarmed*). Where are you going ?

MUM. To get my hat out of the hall. (*She goes into the hall, talking through the door.*) Where are the bridesmaids ? Has your Dad come back yet ? (*She comes back carrying her hat.*)

GWEN. Dad ? No, not a sign of him.

MUM (*putting on her hat at the sideboard mirror*). Don't tell me the groom's going to be late. Mrs Roby was over at your Gran's and she says Jack Orwell and the best man were drinking pints at all the pubs in town last night. That's *one* thing you'll have to put your foot down about.

GWEN. Yes, Mum. (*She conceals the violets hastily in the box.*)

MUM. Have you everything packed ?

GWEN. Yes, Mum.

MUM. I'll lay you've forgotten something. I'd best go up and have a look in your wardrobe.

(*She is about to dash off when* GWEN, *with great presence of mind, gives a heart-rending groan and stages a faint in the fireside chair.*)

GWEN (*loudly*). I'm going to faint. (*She collapses in the chair.*)

MUM (*running to her*). Gwennie ! Love ! Eh, there, there, love ! (*Chafing her hands.*) Have you been reading those nasty books about marriage ?

(*The knocking off* R. *is repeated louder.*)

MUM. Is that someone in the parlour ? (*She drops* GWEN'S *hand and moves a pace towards the door.*)

GWEN (*coming to rather quickly*). Mum—

MUM. It's all right, love. There's someone knocking—(*She moves* R.)

GWEN. It'll be Mavis—practising her Morse Code.

MUM (*checking and turning, at* C.). It's not someone upstairs ?

(GWEN *gives a very loud groan indeed and sinks back in the chair.* MUM *runs to her.*)

GWEN. A—glass of—water.

MUM. Right, love. This minute !

(*She hurries up stage and into the kitchen.* GWEN *sits up.* MAVIS *dashes in* R. *and picks up the parlour key. She signs to* GWEN *that it is all right upstairs, and crosses* R. MUM *dashes in with a glass of water. The knocking becomes louder.*)

MUM (*crossing to* GWEN). What's that hullabaloo, Mavis ?

MAVIS (*at the door*). Polly lying down in the parlour.

MUM. Well, what's she drumming her heels for ? (*To* GWEN.) Here you are, love.

(MAVIS *dashes out to release* POLLY.)

MUM. Lying down, indeed. I hope she had the common sense to take her dress off. Just sip it, love.

(GWEN *sips*. NOTE: *She must leave some in the glass which* MUM *now puts on the table.* POLLY *enters* R., *in her petticoat.* MAVIS *follows carrying her dress.*)

MUM. I'm glad you showed some gumption. Are you better for the lie down?
POLLY. Yes, thanks, Auntie. I feel very nearly well.

(*She takes her dress from* MAVIS, *who moves up* C.)

MUM (*down* L.C.). I suppose that's the nearest we can hope for. Let me help you on with that dress. Come over here, slow coach. (POLLY *crosses to her.*) Up with your arms.

(*They stand in front of* GWEN, *who rises, and moves* R. *above the table, on tip-toe.*)

Stop wriggling. This isn't the shimmy-shake. (*She sees* GWEN.) That's a quick come-round. Where d'you think you're going?

(*She moves* R.C. *to* GWEN, *leaving poor* POLLY *with her dress over her head, concealing her face.*)

GWEN. I forgot—the blue garter for luck.

(*She exits down* R.)

MAVIS (*at the window*). Here's Dad coming up the yard—

(MUM *and* MAVIS *rush to open the back door.* DAD *appears.*)

MUM   } *(together).* { Has the bridegroom left ?
MAVIS   { Who said you could have
my umbrella ?

DAD (*looking over at* POLLY). What the . . . ?

MUM. Mavis ! (*Pointing to* POLLY.) Go over
and unveil the memorial.

(MAVIS *does so.* MUM *takes the umbrella and puts
it just inside the kitchen, talking all the time.*)

I thought you'd fallen in canal the time you took.
It's getting late, you know. Did you see the bridegroom's car ?

DAD. Aye—I saw it. (*He moves to up* C.)

MUM. Well ? What did he say ?

DAD. Nowt. He weren't in it.

MUM (*up* R.C.). He—*what* ?

DAD. The best man gave me this note for Gwennie.

(MUM *sinks into the chair* R. *of the table.* POLLY *is
now in front of the fireside chair.* MAVIS *moves
to* DAD.)

MUM. Open it, someone—open it.

DAD. But it's for Gwen—

MUM. Open it, you moidering idiot—

MAVIS. Give it to me, Dad. (*She takes the note
and opens it.*)

(*Off stage, the dog howls.*)

MUM. What did I tell you ? Listen to that !
Bad Luck ! Go on, read it—

MAVIS (*slowly*). '' Thirty five Wedgewood Street,
Harbiggen, Wednesday.''

MUM (*moaning*). Give me *patience* . . . !

MAVIS. '' Dear Gwen, It's no go. I never wanted
to run Dad's shops for him and I never wanted to
get married.''

MUM (*sitting erect*). The villain ! The black
hearted villain ! I'll have the law on him for this !

MAVIS. " By the time you get this I will be over
the sea and far away "—flown to Douglas, I bet,
the lucky thing—" Forgive me for any suffering I
may have caused to you and yours."

MUM (*cutting in*). That's nowt to the suffering I'll
cause to him and his'n—

MAVIS (*continuing to read*). " With deepest sym-
pathy in your loss—Jack." And then he's crossed
out three kisses. (*She puts the letter on the table.*)

POLLY. Jilted on her wedding day. Oh ! (*She
starts to give at the knees.*)

(DAD *rushes over, and lowers her into the chair above
the fire. Meanwhile* MUM *is working herself up
to hysterics.*)

MUM. I'll sue him, see if I don't ! *And* that
nasty old father of his ! Never did trust him further
than I could throw him ! Making us a byword in the
parish ! If you were half a man, Will Mason, you'd
be following him this minute with a gun—(*She springs
up and paces about.*)

DAD. Where would I get a gun ?

MUM (*turning*). Sneaking and sly, all the Orwells.
Always was. Why has this happened to me ? It's
a judgment on me ! (*Working to below the table.*)
I should never have burned Tom Osborne's letters !
Oh—oh—oh . . . . !

DAD. Mavis ! Some water ! Quick !

(MAVIS *dashes off into the kitchen.*)

Mother—give *over* ! Do you hear me ? Give over !
(*This, with surprising fierceness for* DAD. *He sees the
unfinished glass of water on the table.*) Well—you've
asked for it ! (*He flings the water in* MUM'S *face.*)

MUM (*diminuendo*). Oh !

(POLLY, *furious at being out of the picture, calls
" Mother " and starts to drum her heels.* DAD

*sees there is a drop left in the glass and very casually
flings it in* POLLY'S *surprised face.*)

MUM (*meekly*). Dad—what are we going to do ?
DAD (*giving her a handkerchief*). Wipe your face,
first. You look ridiculous. (*He turns.*) And, Polly,
sit up and behave yourself or I'll give you something
to be sick *about*.

(MAVIS *runs in carrying a basin.*)

DAD. Too late, love. I've revived 'em.
MAVIS. Well, you might have waited for me !
(*She nods towards the back door.*) Open this, will
you ?
DAD (*moving up and doing so*). Where you taking
that water ?
MAVIS. For poor old Podger.

(*She exits.*)

DAD (*closing the door*). Don't tell me the damn
dog's fainted ! (*He crosses to the sideboard.*)
MUM (*wailing*). What are we going to do ? (*Moving about, below the table.*) How are we going to
break it to Gwen ? She'll never be able to raise her
poor little head again—

(DAD *pulls the flowers out of the vase on the sideboard
and raises the vase threateningly.*)

DAD. Steady on, Mother !
MUM. Sorry, Will.
DAD (*enjoying the sound of it*). Say that again.
MUM (*sniffling*). Sorry—Will—(*She moves up,* R.
of the table to above and L. *of it.*)

(GWEN *marches in cheerfully down* R. *and crosses
to the table where she proceeds to look for the
violets in the box.*)

DAD. What are you looking for, Gwennie?

GWEN (*above and* R. *of the table*). Some violets I'm going to carry at my wedding.

POLLY. Wedding! Oh! (*She wails.*)

MUM (*easing down* L. *of the table*). Wedding! O—h! (*She wails louder.*)

DAD (*easing to* R.C.). I've some—bad news for you, love. A letter from Jack—here—read it. (*He hands her the note.*)

(GWEN *reads it, as* DAD *crosses to* MUM. *From this time onwards the sun begins to break through at the window.*)

MUM. We'll never be able to walk down the street again. The taxi due at any moment—all the neighbours waiting—they've talked of nothing else for weeks.

GWEN. When they see who's with me in the taxi they'll talk of nothing else for *years*! (*She calls to* R.) Come in!

(TOM *runs in and stands with his arm round her.*)

MUM. Tom Osborne! The last straw! (*She begins to weep quietly.*)

TOM. That's a fine way to greet your future son-in-law. Cheer up, Ma!

MUM. Ma!

(POLLY *rises.*)

TOM. And stop that snivelling. This is a time for rejoicing. Smile! Go on! Who's to know that your Gwen didn't turn down Jack Orwell at the last minute to marry me? It's Jack who'll look the fool—and Gwen will be the envy of every girl in town. Smile, the lot of you!

(*The front door bell rings, off* R.)

There's the taxi. (*To* POLLY.) Answer it—go on, Dorothy Lamour !

POLLY (*actually hurrying as she crosses* R.). Oh, Mr Osborne, you're so masterful. (*She exits* R.)

TOM. Are you ready, Ma ? We don't want to be late at the Registry Office—

MUM (*horrified*). Registry Office ? (*She goes down* L.) I'll not allow it.

TOM (*moving to below the table with* GWEN). What about those letters of mine you destroyed ? What about this letter from Jack ? (*Picking it up from the table.*) If you don't give your consent—I'll publish this letter in Saturday's *Gazette*. Read all about it. " Bride Deserted at the Church ! "

DAD (*easing down to her*). Now then, Mother, you must let bygones be bygones. The lad's right—come on, love—for our Gwennie's sake—

MUM. But the Vicar—the guests . . . ?

TOM. I've a mate at the Church telling them it's off, and I phoned the Vicar half an hour since.

(POLLY *enters* R., *and goes over to the table to collect her bouquet. She speaks as she crosses.*)

POLLY. There's two taxis at door and Mr Willaby says will you kindly buck up he's got a funeral in half an hour. (*She picks up her flowers and marches to the door* R.) Eh, Gwen, you're a lucky thing. Two bridegrooms in one day.

(*She exits.*)

DAD (*crossing to* GWEN). Gwennie, love. Are you sure this is how you want it ?

GWEN (L. *of* TOM). Yes, Dad—really.

DAD (*turning to* MUM). Come on, Mother. (*He offers her his arm.*)

MUM. I'm not going willing. I've never forgotten how Tom Osborne's Uncle George back worded our—

TOM (*waving the letter*).   Saturday's *Gazette* !

(MUM *shakes off* DAD'S *arm, stalks across* R., *and off.*
DAD *moves to* R.C., *and turns.*)

DAD.   Remember one thing, Tom.   Show who's
boss from the start.

(*He exits.*   TOM *bows to* GWEN, *and offers her his arm.*)

GWEN (*pausing*).   One minute.   You were upstairs.
How did you know what was in Jack Orwell's letter ?
TOM.   Well—I ran across him in a pub last night.
I never saw a fellow more miserable in all my life.
GWEN (*laughing*).   Thanks for the compliment.
TOM.   It seems his Dad's been nattering at him to
settle down and he never has liked working in those
shops and—and . . . (*He breaks off, a little nervously.*)
GWEN.   Tom Osborne.   Did you dictate that
letter to him ?
TOM.   Not exactly, love.   But I did happen to
mention that if he so much as showed his face this
morning I'd break every—well, it wouldn't be healthy.
GWEN.   Tom !   You're so reckless—so impulsive
—are we going to be happy ?

(TOM *runs up to the back door and flings it open.   The
sun streams through.*)

TOM.   You'll never regret it, Gwen.   Look—I've
even made the sun shine for you.   And " Happy
is the Bride that the Sun Shines on."
GWEN.   Oh, Tom . . .

(*He comes down and takes her in his arms.   Off* R. *a
taxi sounds its horn impatiently.   The lovers break
away to listen.   There is a frightful commotion in
the backyard as if someone has knocked the dustbin
over.   Through the back door comes an excited dog
with a white ribbon on its collar and on the end of*

its lead a panting MAVIS. *They go down to the door* R.)

Mavis ! You're not bringing that dog to the Registry Office.

MAVIS. Registry Office be blowed. We're off to Heckleydown Dog Show. (*Quick exit.*)

(*She dashes off. The lovers laugh. They kiss. The taxi horn sounds again and again. They take no notice.*)

CURTAIN.

FURNITURE AND PROPERTY LIST

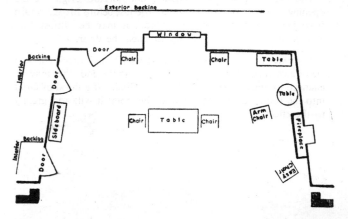

Carpet on stage. Rug at hearth. Strip in hall. Curtains at window.

On the walls : Suitable pictures for the type of room.

1 sideboard. *On it :* Usual dressings. A vase of flowers.

1 small kitchen table. *On it :* Coloured tablecloth. A florist's box containing a bridal bouquet, a bridesmaid's bouquet, and a floral shoulder spray. A milliner's box containing a hat as described in the play.

4 small chairs. (*Set as in plan.*)

1 armchair. 1 small easy chair. 1 occasional table, with plant.

1 side table (*up* L.) or cupboard.

Fender and fire-irons.

On the mantelpiece : Clock. Ornaments. Match-holder. A small jeweller's box containing bracelets as described in the play.

Ready off up R. (*in kitchen*) : A glass of water. (*Extra water for re-filling.*) A bowl.

Ready off down R. (*in the hall*) : A spray of violets wrapped in cellophane, with card.
Raincoat, " pixie ", black umbrella, and coloured ditto.

TOM : A letter in an envelope.

MRS BAGSHAW : Umbrella—wet. Raincoat—wet.

NOTE ON THE LIGHTING

The lighting must be adequate, but not too bright at the opening. It may be brought up a little just before MUM's return from her mother. Towards the end, it may be almost full, and quite full as TOM goes up to open the door.

The exterior backing should be flooded No. 17 Steel, checked well down through most of the play. At the end, this may be changed to mingled White and No. 51 Gold. If a flood of Gold into the room can be provided at this point it will add greatly to the effect.